T0062743

HE
LEADETH
ME

Charlotte Halsell Bradshaw

Inspiring Voices

Copyright © 2014 Charlotte Halsell Bradshaw.

All rights reserved. No part of this book may be used or reproduced by
any means, graphic, electronic, or mechanical, including photocopying,
recording, taping or by any information storage retrieval system
without the written permission of the publisher except in the case
of brief quotations embodied in critical articles and reviews.

Inspiring Voices books may be ordered through booksellers or by contacting:

Inspiring Voices
1663 Liberty Drive
Bloomington, IN 47403
www.inspiringvoices.com
1 (866) 697-5313

Because of the dynamic nature of the Internet, any web addresses or
links contained in this book may have changed since publication and
may no longer be valid. The views expressed in this work are solely those
of the author and do not necessarily reflect the views of the publisher,
and the publisher hereby disclaims any responsibility for them.

Any people depicted in stock imagery provided by Thinkstock are
models, and such images are being used for illustrative purposes only.
Certain stock imagery © Thinkstock.

ISBN: 978-1-4624-1049-1 (sc)

Printed in the United States of America.

Inspiring Voices rev. date: 09/15/2014

DEDICATION AND ACKNOWLEDGEMENTS

This book is dedicated to the love of my
late husband of fifty-nine years, JD.

I would also like to acknowledge my
father, mother, and sister who gave me
a happy home and childhood.

.....and my own children and their families
who have given me tremendous love and
support in all my activities including working
computer magic by a son-in-law and a
daughter who served as photographer.

INTRODUCTION

This book "He Leadeth Me" has been written to describe the many ways God has led my life from age seventeen. It was not always apparent at the time, but as I look back, I see God's guiding hand. I consider this relationship with God to be the most important influence in my being able to "Wake Up and Smile". hope this will encourage others to enjoy life and join me in the enthusiasm to start each day with a smile.

The biblical quotations have been carefully chosen from the King James version of the Bible to represent the promises God has made that have guided my life throughout the past seventy years.

Matthew 7:7 "Ask, and it shall be given you; seek, and ye shall find; knock, and it shall be opened unto you:" offers the same leadership to anyone who desires it.

I would like to invite anyone who reads this book and relates to the leadership of God to email me at windsorrn@gmail.com and describe your experience with being led by God. Your response will be permission to use your story, not your name, in my next book, "He Will Lead You, too". Looking forward to YOUR story.

CHAPTER 1

"Trust in the Lord with all thine heart; and
lean not unto thine own understanding. In
all thy ways acknowledge Him, and He shall
direct thy paths." Proverbs 3: 5,6 KJV

I met God in a little farmhouse in the San Joaquin
Valley. I knew there was a God, but I had left Him sitting
comfortably up on the shelf until I visited some cousins
in the Valley one summer. Our family motored up to visit
my grandfather and Mother and Dad stayed with him.
My sister and I split up, and she went to an uncle's home.
I was shipped off to a cousin I admired, which was my
choice.

I was only seven but the picture is vivid in my mind
of a Mother, Maud, Father, Shelby and a daughter, Shelly
Ann, who was ten years my senior. I liked to stay with

them because Shelly and I were privileged to sleep in the tank house. The tank house was a room up over a storage tank that I guess contained their water supply. I never questioned what was below us. I was just excited to be up high where we could look out over the valley and be closer to the stars.

They lived in a quaint little farmhouse and we all gathered in the homey living room for bedtime devotions. Maud read from the Bible. Shelby, Shelly and I sat quietly listening. The scripture and prayers have long been forgotten, but not the deep feeling of God's love and presence that permeated the room.

This was a unique family that had learned to overcome the hardships of ill-health and thank God for each other. Maud was a school teacher which paid for their livelihood. She was strong, dependable and devoted to her family. Shelly Ann was a lovely young girl who radiated being loved and loving her life.

Even as a child, though, I recognized the strength of Shelby--that is, spiritual strength, for of physical strength he had very little. He was a slight man. When he stood, he was barely my height--being bent nearly double with his head in line with his waist. His arms dangled uselessly at his sides. Periodically, for a change of position, Maud or Shelly would grasp each of his hands and pull him to a standing position where he remained for a short time and then was lowered in the same manner, again to his chair. His every move, including feeding, was done for him. His only independent movement was a constant palsy with arms shaking uncontrollably. I had to listen very closely to understand his soft, hesitant speech, but there was one thing his handicapped condition had not dimmed. He had a twinkle in his eye that seemed to mirror a strong and courageous soul brimming with the love of God and his family.

In this brief evening devotion, I was introduced to God as a constant friend, comforter, and healer of the soul. That was only an introduction, and at my young age I did not pursue Him as a regular companion. The God I would later meet and follow His leading, just went back on the shelf for a few more years

We returned to our daily living--our family of four-- Mother, Grace, Father, Charles, sister, Connie and I was three and a half years younger. America was just coming out of the Great Depression with all it's hardships and was now in World War II and rationing. Mother was a true stay-at-home mom and my Father was an early entrepreneur whose job might consist of cracking walnuts for a candy store, making hominy, mustard pickles or vanilla to barter at the Tradex Store, or off to the mountains to pan for gold that was claimed to be in "them thar hills". In good times he was a salesman for the cemetery where he made around a hundred dollars a month to care for our family. Thanks to my great uncle who was more prosperous than Dad, we always had a roof over our heads. My sister and I often marvel at the fact that we didn't know we were poor.

The Tradex, I mentioned, was a unique invention born out of the depression for people with no money but tradable resources. Each person brought whatever they could scrape together and traded it for anything someone else had to offer. Each visit brought surprises. Mother became the proud possessor of a large braided rag rug that graced their bedroom for years. Once Dad brought me a pair of red and white striped pajamas, but my biggest prize was a new? bed. This was a real bed with head, foot, springs and mattress. Quite an upgrade from the canvas army cot I had slept on since outgrowing the crib. I was thrilled. Tradex also helped provide the essentials of simple food.

One summer we spent in the mountains at Big Bear. We thought we had become members of the rich and famous to have a mountain retreat. Years later we found that it was a time Dad was out of work and he was seriously hunting for gold. We stayed in a rustic mountain cabin owned by some unknown person. We didn't see a "No trespassing sign" so we just enjoyed it. There could have been some other arrangements that I didn't know about. I think we could have been called "squatters", but we had a wonderful, memorable vacation. We stayed all summer. We even thought the cheap creamed codfish was great. As for the gold mining, Dad found a nugget worth about five dollars at that time, otherwise, the finds were very small, just tiny pieces of gold called colors.

It was ten years later when I heard the declaration, "You have been chosen to receive the scholarship funds for a week at Methodist Girls' Camp". It was 1944. The camp was in the beautiful San Bernardino mountains and the funds were given by Maud O. Yes, that was the Maud whose evening devotion had so impressed me at the age of seven. She hadn't known that I was going to be the recipient of that fifteen dollar gift. That proclamation placed my feet on the trail up the mountain where I was to make the most important decision of my life.

I was seventeen years old and just graduated from high school. For several years my friends had returned from camp with stories of the great time they had at summer camp, but fifteen dollars was always beyond our family's budget.

When the day to leave for camp arrived, I had no idea how my life was about to change. The August weather was beautiful and Camp Radford, an established campground, was lovely. To me, being in the mountains was close to my picture of heaven. We received our cabin assignments and the schedule for the week. Our greatest experience was the opportunity to have fellowship and guidance from the missionaries. These dedicated people had been all over the world working for many years telling and showing God's love. They had worked in mission fields for most of their lives and just radiated the love of God.

Our week climaxed on the last night at a fire circle with a devotion. Then it was our turn to look within our own minds and feelings and write ourselves a letter which was placed at the foot of a small cross of branches and would be mailed to us after returning home.

I had been raised in a Christian home and had attended church longer that I could remember. I was placed on the Cradle Roll before I was a month old, but my personal relationship with God had remained with Him on the shelf. However, after that night, He came down off the shelf to be a real and trusted close friend who would be with me constantly to guide me everyday. What a concept! This is a copy of the letter I penned to my self on August 3, 1944 and received January 1945.

"Dear God from a rededicated Christian,
I have made a decision tonight to
discipline my life when
I get home to be a better Christian.
This has been a beautiful experience among all the trees
and mountains that God has made.

I want to go home and work to
bring more people to thee.
I want to let my light shine so
others can see Jesus in me.
With the help of God I want to do
these things and have a
quiet time with Him everyday so that
I may talk to Him and listen
for His answers, and to read my Bible
and learn more about Him
so I may tell others. I want to walk in His footsteps.
I pledge my life to Thee, Lord, and
ask you to do with it in
Thine own way.
Help me to be a good Christian and do Thy will.
Help me to have love and peace in my heart.
In all faith which I have in God I ask these things
and pledge myself to Him."

I have kept this letter for these nearly 70 years and the inspiration I gleaned from that week at camp has guided me in accepting God as my personal leader in all of life. During this time of soul searching and dedication I also made another decision that I had not anticipated.

As long as I could remember, I had only one career in mind and that was to be a nurse--I couldn't imagine any obstacle to get in my way short of dying. My lifelong friend, June, and I had researched all the possibilities and found that since we were in the war, the government had established the Cadet Nurse Corps which provided the training, including books, instruction in a hospital, and a small stipend, with the stipulation you remain in nursing for the duration and six months. We found the Huntington Memorial Hospital in Pasadena, California, offered this program. We had received their brochure and followed the prerequisites one by one since our sophomore year in high school. We needed our one year of junior college and then we would be ready to begin the exciting career we had chosen

I had no idea of changing my focus. However, in September 1943 my sister's boyfriend, Leland, who was in the Navy brought along a sailor friend, JD, who was expected to be my date. We got along well and had a good time and Leland was so enthused he told JD, "You are going to marry that girl". JD thought that was a little ridiculous because he was 25 and I was only 16.

JD did ask if he could come again and I said "Sure". He came back and continued to come back every week and we enjoyed our time together. By April he talked of marriage but knew I was determined to go into nursing so he didn't press the issue. I had never given him an answer but we just enjoyed the present. By this time, age did not seem to be a factor. All of the boys looked young especially in uniform. The Navy particularly. I have always been partial to cute little boys in sailor suits, and I guess I was born "old". Therefore we ended up about the same age. JD did get promoted to Chief Radioman so he wore an officer uniform instead of the sailor one after that.

During my time at camp, JD wrote to me every day. I realized I really looked forward to his letters and how much he had become a special part of my life. In fact, while I was making decisions I decided that he was the person I wanted to spend the rest of my life with but.... not yet.

Upon my return home, we discussed the future at length and agreed that he needed to finish his time in the Navy, which was undecided as long as the war continued, and then he expected to go to college on the G.I.Bill which would pay for school because of his Navy time. And besides I had one more year of college and three years of training. We were looking at a long wait, but we knew we could do it together--although separately.

June and I completed all our classes in college, anatomy, physiology, bacteriology, chemistry and not to forget the required P.E. class. The only one we could squeeze in was natural dancing. Now I was not named "Grace" for a reason. My Mother's name was Grace, but

I did not fit the picture. As for flitting around the floor in our short little billowy skirts, that was just not me. However, anything for the cause, so we suffered and endured the semester and came out with blushing cheeks and stupid embarrassed grins and tried to pretend it never happened.

The new Santa Ana Junior College had not been built at that time so we had to walk several blocks from one building to another. Our anatomy class was right before lunch in a classroom across from the YMCA. As soon as we finished doing our dissecting with hands still smelling of formaldehyde, we dashed over to the "Y" for a hamburger. We were so anxious to get all our units completed we were not bothered about adding a little obnoxious smell to our lunch and the other customers didn't seem to mind.

We found we could not begin in June as planned because the required nutrition class would only be given in the summer session. We completed that and finally were ready to go into the September nursing class at Huntington Hospital.

Not quite so fast. One little obstacle. Before that day arrived, the whole country took to the streets in celebration. We heard the newsboys on every corner crying, "Extra, Extra. Read all about it. WAR IS OVER!" There was no TV saying, "Breaking News". News came through the newspaper printing extra editions for big news or over the radio. We were all so excited we just stampeded down Main Street and gathered in the middle of Santa Ana at Fourth and Main. That was the end of World War II on August 14, 1945.

When the excitement settled down, we needed to examine the obstacle. Would they still have the Cadet Nurse Corps since the war was over? How would we pay for the training if they didn't? Amid all of our questions and prayers our answer came. I just knew that we would become nurses some way, but I had no idea how, but God was one step ahead of us. The Cadet Nurse Corps was ending, but the September class would be the final group of students. We were so excited we could barely contain ourselves. We anxiously waited for September to arrive so we could become members of the Cadet Nurse Corps.

JD was discharged from the Navy in August as soon as the war ended, so he made plans to begin college just in time for the fall semester. June and I began our classes on September 7.

It was not long before JD phoned to tell me he had found a place to live while going to USC. He had headed for UCLA but got off the track and ended up at USC so applied there. Surprise! He was now living across town with a room in a house with an older couple. It looked like an ideal situation but ground rules were already set up by the nursing department. We had to be in our rooms by 8:00PM so that didn't allow for any shirking of our duties for dating. That was good and we were both busy in our respective endeavors. We appreciated the rare times we could see one another, and it was nice to know he wasn't far away.

Every week I made a mad dash to catch the Short Line Streetcar from Pasadena to Los Angeles (L.A.) and the streamliner from L.A. to Santa Ana on my day off. I looked forward to JD meeting me at the train depot on my return and taking me back to the nurse's residence.

When our enforced early curfew seemed too soon to part, JD who was a radioman from a way back relied on his morse code and a flashlight to blink out this message to my second floor room ".. ._.. _ _ _ ..._ . _._ _ _ _ _ .. _ " which I had learned said, "I love you".That was a unique and lovely way to say goodnight.

One week I arrived in L.A. and found I had missed the train. I went to a telephone booth (long before they had cell phones) to call home and tell them I would be taking the streetcar instead of the train. Then I walked over to catch the next streetcar to Santa Ana. When I went to buy the ticket, I found I had no wallet. Oh my, here I am in the middle of L.A. without a cent to my name. I figured I would just trust to the kindness of the conductor, so I boarded the streetcar as if I knew what

I was doing. When the man came by to collect tickets, I didn't cry like I would have liked to but told him my sad story and said, "If you will give me your name and address, I will mail you the fare". With a sympathetic half smile he did just that and I proceeded homeward. Of course, when I arrived in Santa Ana, I still had to get home so I went to the cab office and when the driver delivered me home, I just asked him to wait and I ran in to get the money from my mother. My father always had told me that," God looks out for fools and orphans". I'm so glad that God has provided all the angels to care for us in the unorphan category. When I returned to Pasadena a man from South Pasadena phoned to say he had found my wallet in a telephone booth, and if I would come down there he would return it to me. I hopped on another streetcar and thankfully retrieved my misplaced wallet.

Nurses' training was not limited to taking temperatures and blood pressures and holding the patient's hand. There was much to learn. The instructors were not only teaching but were excellent role models. Having students at the hospital was an advantage to the institution. We worked from 7 to 12 and 3:30 to 7 with classes in between 12 and 3. The schedule covered the busiest hours of the day. We gave baths and backrubs to everyone and used this time for observation and assessment to be charted and shared at daily report.

Time passed quickly as we were immersed in the busy schedule. We moved from one floor assignment to another from medical, to surgical, to pediatrics to maternity and orthopedics and out patient clinic. We were sent to other affiliating hospitals, to Orange County for communicable diseases, to Hollywood Children's for pediatrics and Compton for psychiatric. Compton was the place I spent my 21st birthday--in a mental institution. A memorable experience of having chairs thrown at me, swinging doors threatening to knock me over and being called unprintable names which would now be considered "politically incorrect" and the only time I ever resorted to walking in my sleep.

JD and I often dreamed about the time when we would be married, but returned to reality when we listed all that had to be done before that great day would arrive. We decided, though, to make it seem more real we could officially become engaged. We had been counting down the years-four more, three more, and were at two more the last September, and it was now February so only about one and a half to go. We thought that was a good plan.

On February 11, 1947, JD phoned and asked if he could come over. I had a student meeting to attend, but I said, "OK but not for long". He apparently was so excited that he took off a piece of the garage as he was backing out in his '37 Dodge. He picked me up and we drove to

El Molina Park and found a romantic spot. With all the sophistication he could muster, he asked me to marry him and presented me with a diamond ring. In my own excitement I managed a "Yes". Now we were officially betrothed. Then he took me back to my meeting.

Time seemed to be moving along fairly quickly. JD found an ad in the paper selling a small house in a court. They were selling the 20x20 houses on 40x40 lots each separately and at a price he could afford with his severance pay he had saved from his Navy discharge. He proudly made the big purchase.

One more rung up the ladder. I had graduation at the Rose Bowl in June. We wouldn't actually finish until September, but all of Pasadena had one big ceremony. We wore our white uniforms for a day and then back to the blue and white students' garb. JD finished with his B.A, degree in August. He completed his four years in three so we could come out even. With our last vacation I was home sewing curtains, drapes, and bedspread for the house. JD had stayed at the new house even without furniture so saved rent money. He had splurged at the thrift store and now we would have a new? iron, toaster and even a stove. I think they were the finest that came over on the Mayflower but it was wonderful--progressing! Anything that didn't work he could always repair so that was not a problem. When we really moved in, the furniture in the house consisted of a bed, a dresser brought from my house, an overstuffed chair from someone's throw away, a table and one chair from my house, an antique stove that leaked gas, and a very old refrigerator. That was it for several months.

Everything was working out just as we had been planning with God always leading the way these last five years. We had met on Saturday, September 18, 1943 and we set the marriage date for Saturday, September 18, 1948. I finished at Huntington on the 7th and then went home to wait for the Day. On the 16th JD came for our last date. We went to Knott's Berry Farm and then had two more days of anticipation, he in Pasadena and I in Santa Ana. We had purchased our marriage license and were planning with only my family (his Mother was in Oklahoma) to be married by Reverend Karl Heilman at his Methodist Church in Upland, California. Rev. Heilman was our minister for nine years in Santa Ana while we were going together.

When I wakened Saturday morning, the 18th, the world was beautiful and I felt gorgeous (except for an itchy mosquito bite on my leg) in my new maroon colored suit with grey accessories, including hat and gloves. My Mother, Father, sister and I were soon on our way to Upland for a 10 o'clock wedding. When we arrived, JD was already there. He had come early and had breakfast in Upland so he wouldn't be late.

Rev. Heilman had everything ready including the organist playing. I have no idea what pieces she played. By that time I was not sure of my own name. We stood at the altar with Connie as my maid of honor and my Dad as JD's best man. The ceremony began. I guess I said my "I do's" at the proper time. My voice was barely audible as I replied, with tears of happy, streaming down my cheeks and clutching JD's hand. Then the minister said, "You may kiss the bride". As JD kissed me, all I could think of was, "We finally made it! Just think, someday we will have a Golden Anniversary".

That was the most beautiful wedding I can imagine. We thought we were the happiest couple on the planet and remained so for the next almost fifty-nine years. We had waited for this day for five busy years, but never regretted the things we accomplished in that time, however, five years can be a v-e-r-y l-o-n-g time.

JD so aptly summarized the wedding ceremony, saying, "When Reverend Heilman solemnizes it, it is REALLY solemn".

CHAPTER 2

"Train up a child in the way he should
go and when he is old he will not
depart from it" Proverbs 22:6 KJV

We returned from our overnight honeymoon at Mt. Wilson and JD carried me over the threshold to enter our new home. A king and queen might have a gigantic, luxurious palace but they couldn't be more happy than we were with our little three room sparsely furnished bungalow next to the railroad tracks in Pasadena. On the other side of the tracks a couple of blocks away was the elite area of the city. It made beautiful scenery for a stroll but no desire to live there.

We felt blessed to have our home, JD had been hired to teach school in east L.A. I would be working at Huntington Hospital in the newborn nursery and studying to take State Board exams in November. He, of course, worked days, but I would be on 3--11PM shift. My classmates had given us a pressure cooker for a wedding present, and JD became proficient in cooking our evening meal. I could dash down the railroad tracks, and he would have dinner prepared. There was just time to eat and then run back to work. He even cleaned the kitchen and washed the dishes--married life was good.

God had guided me through the last five years and I had faith He would continue. I needed all the help I could get to pass State Board exams in November. That was an experience I would not like to have to repeat. This was a year of transition. The exam had been a one day event, but this year it was changed to three days. I studied diligently knowing this was a Big Exam--a culmination of all we had learned the last three years.

I joined my classmates in the trip to L.A. to take the exam in November and had no word until January. When the letter finally arrived, I held my breath and with trembling hands tore open the envelope. Wonder of wonders, I PASSED and I could now sign the charts with RN after my name. This day would go down in history as a red letter day.

Since I didn't get home until about midnight, JD went to bed earlier as he had to be up for school the next day. One night I came home to a quiet house except for a hissing sound. Our hot water tank was quite small and manually lighted each time to get hot water. The trick was to remember to turn it off when you finished a bath. Apparently JD forgot that last function and now the water was BOILING. The next thing would be to blow through the roof. Realizing what the hissing was I quickly roused JD who immediately jumped out of bed-I never saw him move so fast. We turned off the burner and opened every water faucet in our three room house. In a very short time you couldn't see your hand in front of your face for the steam. We opened doors and windows and finally cleared out the fog--problem solved and we didn't even call 911, which was unheard of at that time. It was good that I hadn't worked overtime or we might have had to do some fancy repairs. Newlyweds do need divine protection and guidance to help them reach their fiftieth anniversary.

There was no way to be sure, but we had hopes that the next step was going to be adding to our family. We were happy to announce at Christmas time that my folks were going to be grandparents in July. With that knowledge came the search to trade our happy little honeymoon cottage for a larger house with a yard and room for a child to grow.

Tract homes had just begun to spring up around the country, so we began searching. We had thought our destination would eventually be Orange County where my parents lived. The closest we came was Norwalk. Then to be able to qualify for the loan was to be considered. We were very conservative and knew we could live quite frugally but the loan experts have their own figures. We found that if we used both our salaries we could qualify. However, time was of the essence because in my condition my time of having a salary was limited. All worked out well, and we signed for a new three bedroom home on Harvest Avenue in Norwalk with a monthly payment of $77.00. At that time it was a fair amount of the monthly income. We were able to sell our little house with a slight profit and move by April. Again God guided our decisions and the outcomes.

New houses had no amenities like carpet, air conditioning, washer, dryer, or landscaping, only the bare necessities. One of the first things to buy was an incinerator. Every back yard had a place to burn trash. That was before pollution was a common word. JD transferred to his construction mode and built a concrete block wall enclosing the back yard. We looked for bargains for baby furniture and we had a Maytag wringer washing machine that my Mother had outgrown. Carpet was not considered a necessity.

JD had finished his year of teaching and was not planning to return to the school. In fact, by this time he was disillusioned with teaching. It had been a very difficult year. It was an assignment for a seasoned teacher not a first year rookie. He was a radioman in the Navy and had a longtime interest in radio that progressed to TV so he readily found a job with RCA Television in Lynwood, which was close by. He was the man who climbed on the roof to install your antenna.

JD's Mother came out from Oklahoma for the blessed event. We would be traveling back to Pasadena for the delivery, so we hoped to allow enough time. There were no freeways but surface streets carried us to the hospital with twelve hours to spare.

Our baby, Karla, arrived as expected in July and, we were so happy to now be a family of three. She was named for Karl Heilman, the minister who performed our wedding ceremony. He was very proud of that namesake.

Karla was such a joy, we added a little brother, Roy, two years later. The end of the next year, just before Christmas, Corrine also joined the family. I said I wanted twelve children so we had a good start. I think I must have been delusional.

Our plans now were to move out where the children would have room to run and we could have chickens, rabbits, dogs, cats, lions, tigers and maybe elephants. Maybe not the last three, but we did want lots of room. We searched the newspapers each week when we visited my parents. JD had purchased a book, "Five Acres and Security". That book gave us all kinds of ideas--maybe build a garage and live in it while we built a house, or maybe build a house on an acre or two of land. Most of the prices of acreage were beyond our budget, and we were not ones to have a large debt, so we just kept looking.

One day an ad caught our eyes and it looked like it might fulfill our dream. We called the real estate agent. He was busy with a family birthday party so he couldn't show us the place but he gave us an address. It was in the county area between Santa Ana and Garden Grove. I had lived all my life in Santa Ana but had never heard of Clinton Avenue. We had also been given directions so we eagerly drove by on our way back to Norwalk. It was an older house built in 1927, cape cod style with upstairs windows, had a large area between the houses on either side and had a partial picket fence. There was an orange grove across the way and on down both sides of the street. There were no sidewalks, and the road was only paved in the center for cars to travel. It looked very "out in the country". When we got home, we phoned the agent and asked for an appointment to see the house the next day. We were so excited we talked far into the night and hardly slept the hours we had left. Is it possible? What is the inside like? How big is it? What is out back? Questions, questions, we could hardly wait.

The next evening we packed up the children and dropped them off with the grand parents. We were so anxiously anticipating this meeting. Could it possibly live up to our brief view? On our arrival Mr. Berry escorted us into the house. The living room walls were painted a ghastly, dark green as was the style at that time, but there was a fireplace. The house was built in a U shape and then later a 17x18 room enclosed the U and made a den, which was packed sky high with furniture belonging to the owner, (there had been renters the last four years). The former chicken ranch had left evidence in the black fly specks profusely covering the venetian blinds. There was a very tall antenna in the back yard. The owner had used the room upstairs over the garage for a radio shack transmitting messages to and from service people overseas during the war. The room was very "rustic", and that is a nice way of saying it was barely presentable. There were only two bedrooms in the house, and we had three children. The one bathroom was at least indoors. The upstairs windows were only for design. It was on a commercial acre of land. "It was perfect"!!!!

A few gallons and several coats of paint would cover the green, the owners surely would remove the excess furniture, soap and water could erase the fly specks, the children were small yet and one bedroom was workable or we could divide the large den if necessary. We had never had more than one bathroom. The antenna could come down and the upstairs over the garage we could think about later. There was lots of room out back to do whatever we wanted and there was a grape arbor. "We'll take it" We eagerly signed on the dotted line and gave a deposit. There were times when we were surprised where God chose to lead us, but happy we'd been led.

We didn't even know yet that in a few years this Cape Cod style would prove useful. Those windows upstairs were perfect after JD built a rather steep stairway through a bedroom closet and finished the upstairs into two bedrooms. He also, I helped a little, finished the upstairs over the garage into a nice apartment and added a complete bathroom. JD claimed this bathroom as his, so he didn't have to share the other one. It was a little tricky when it rained to go outside and upstairs, but this wasn't entirely a new pattern for him. He grew up without all the modern conveniences. This property had just been waiting for us to discover it, or so it seemed.

Our tract home in Norwalk sold readily for about an even trade for the acre and home in Garden Grove. So after four years we were off again for a new adventure. The move went smoothly other than the top flying off the refrigerator on the freeway. It still functioned and only looked kind of funny with a caved in top but served us well for several more years.

JD was so thrilled with our place I think he must have stopped everyone he met on the street to tell them how wonderful it was, as if they really cared. We thought we had something in common with Christopher Columbus. He discovered America, and we discovered Clinton Avenue.

We purchased some chickens and cages and soon had eggs for us and some to sell. We had brought Betsy Rabbit from Norwalk and thought she might like a friend so adopted Mary to keep her company. It wasn't long before we changed Betsy's name to Bertram and made room for all their little bunnies. We were getting to feel like real "country folk".

Five years had passed since I had been active in nursing. I spent those years having children and now needed to get back into my other profession--nursing. I wasn't sure where I could sandwich in the time. Having babysitters was not one of our options.

With a great deal of prayerful thought, I came to the conclusion that there were four hours I could use, although a 7-11PM shift was unheard of. I made an appointment with Sister Philomene at St Joseph Hospital in Orange, not far away.

Sister Philomene greeted me warmly and I explained my proposal. She looked quite skeptically at me and replied, "We do not usually have that kind of position". I agreed with her but suggested maybe there might be more admittances than expected or someone could become ill midshift. In her own quiet way she accepted my explanation and said she would think about it.

Before long, it became a fairly frequent occurrence to have the phone ring in the middle of the afternoon and someone would ask me to come to work. JD arrived home regularly about 6:00PM so he took over the household duties consisting mostly of putting the children to bed, and I was free to keep up with nursing. I worked wherever the need was so was considered a floater and therefore familiar with all the floors. That routine lasted many years and was ideal for us.

One night I was working in the nursery and Sister Paul Francis approached us with the news that a baby boy with Down Syndrome and been delivered. She continued to explain that the parents had been advised not to keep the child but find someone else to care for him. This is a difficult concept to understand but the priest, doctors, and friends all agreed this was the "best" thing to do. I immediately said, "I'll take him". That was a quick decision but one we never regretted. Rather than take him to their home, I met his parents and received Tommy and all his belongings at the hospital. He became our adorable baby instead of the long awaited and joyfully anticipated child of his real parents, who were lovely people and became very good friends of ours. I know they were doing the best they could.

Today this thought process is so different. Parents finally began to realize that although there are distinctive characteristics, the number of chromosomes is only a matter of a name for a syndrome and does not change the miracle that any baby represents. Tommy's parents retained an interest in him and provided for his welfare by paying us $150.00 a month but we reaped the reward of his presence in our family. We all loved him and our two year old daughter began her lifelong career of caring for babies with tirelessly picking up his toys for him as she would a new baby brother.

We did not appreciate yet that Tommy was an angel sent to care for us. We just knew that God had sent us another child. I kept reminding the children, and also myself, that this was only a temporary arrangement. Tommy was just our baby between birth and two years of age. We loved Tommy as if he was our own. We encouraged him but his little legs did not have the strength to be able to walk or crawl. His total vocabulary consisted of one word. What could be sweeter than having a baby look at you with serious soulful eyes and call you "Mama"? He was a special child.

After two years of age, the state would accept a child. He did leave us when he was two and was placed in an institution. It was only a short time later that he developed a viral infection, and our little visiting angel returned to his heavenly home.

CHAPTER 3

"Casting all your care upon Him for He
careth for you". 1 Peter 5:7 KJV

We knew God was always caring for us but didn't know
He was going to be so busy as He was in 1955. January
ended with a telegram that JD's Mother had passed away
in Oklahoma from a sudden heart attack. JD and two
of his brothers, Glenn and Harold immediately made
preparations and drove to their hometown, Boynton,
Oklahoma where his Mother had been living. This was
the first time we had spent a night apart since we were
married. That was a lonely time, but I did have four
children to keep me company and it was only a preview of
what was to come. Although JD had been away from home
for many years he missed his frequent correspondence
with his mother. and just knowing she was there.

JD was only gone for about a week then he returned to work at RCA. Climbing up and down ladders at work was becoming more and more painful due to arthritis in his right hip. By May it became evident that surgery was the only answer, and JD had part of his hip joint replaced with a prosthesis. Total hip replacement had not been discovered yet.

The surgery was performed at Long Beach Veterans' Hospital. He was in a body cast and transported himself on a gurney using his arms to navigate. We thought a few days were long for him to be away and found six weeks to be almost unbearable. My parents helped with the children and I made the trip to Long Beach once or twice a day for what seemed like forever.

Financially we were hitting bottom. Compensation from work was supposed to come forth but the gears turn slowly and a family could starve before that was begun. Our only income was what we had from caring for Tommy, but that was barely enough to sustain four children and myself.

Things were looking better, however. I visited JD one day with an exciting announcement. I had a job that I could do at home. A neighbor had approached me with an inquiry of where they might hire someone to do ironing. They had three little boys and needed some help.

I jumped at the prospect of a job and offered my services, seeing relief in sight for our lack of funds.

I received the first large stack of clothes to iron. After putting the children to bed, I set up the ironing board and turned on the TV and happily went to work. They picked up those clothes and brought another supply so I repeated the process the next day. After the third day of ironing far into the night, the neighbor gathered that last bundle with the promise to pay me the next day. I waited anxiously for the anticipated check the next morning, but to my surprise, I found they had moved during the night and made no provision for paying their bills. That adventure was a disaster, but we survived. It was funny after I recovered from the first shock. For years if anyone suggested making extra money, the answer was, "Take in ironing. You'll make a fortune".

The meager compensation from RCA did finally come through. Still the Veteran's Hospital was attempting to rehabilitate JD for a more suitable job and kept giving him tests. He didn't really feel he needed rehabilitation, just discharge him so he could come home and I could go to work.

Discharge day arrived after six weeks. He had been long enough post op that he was able to care for the children and I went to work full time 3 to 11PM on the medical floor at St Joseph. We could see God's handiwork in guiding me to that unheard of 7 to 11 shift a while back. It was easy to just shift from part time to full time.

We settled into a new kind of routine. JD's brother and family came to visit in August. They took Karla and Roy to the newly opened Disneyland. JD wasn't quite up to it and I was working, but the children had such a good time. Roy was so excited he had gone to the moon. He explained that they hadn't really gone to the moon in case we would think they had.

Just before the visitors left, Roy got up from a nap complaining that his back hurt. Thinking he had probably slept crooked we weren't too concerned and then he started vomiting. This did not subside so I took him to the doctor. She thought it was the flu, but said she was to be gone over Labor Day and if it did not improve to check with another pediatrician.

It did not improve so I chose the most thorough doctor I knew from working in the nursery. He checked Roy and then said what turned my world upside down, "I feel a mass". He immediately made an appointment with a surgeon.

Doctors Engleman and Mears the two best surgeons at St. Joseph's Hospital admitted Roy for exploratory surgery September 9, 1955. We didn't have a definitive diagnosis, but as I talked to Dr. Mears the night before surgery, he was fairly certain what the outcome would be.

When he said Roy might not even come out of surgery or maybe would last only a little longer, all I could do was go over to my parents home and cry because I couldn't fall apart in front of the children.

There was no provision for parents to stay at the hospital with a child so I did finally go home and left Roy with a wonderful nurse with whom I had worked many times. She phoned us and let Roy talk to us and he was fine.

JD and I prayed together and later when I again prayed and then rose from my knees, I suddenly had a feeling of peace and knowing that, although I did not know the outcome, everything was going to be all right. God would care for us.

The exploratory surgery confirmed that it was a lymphosarcoma, a cancer that had metastasized throughout his abdomen. We didn't know how or why. That was it, and there was nothing more they could do. He was discharged in a few days.

We couldn't do NOTHING. Our minister, Rev. Deshler, went with us to take Roy to a faith healer who was having services close by. We did have faith and were hoping for a miracle. There was no change.

A nurse friend told us about a clinic in Texas that was said to have success with cancer. JD and I flew with Roy down to Dallas. Roy was checked at the clinic and given some alternative type medication of vinegar and fruit juices and we returned home the next day.

Roy was weak but was able to be up and about. He looked forward to Karla coming home from first grade to entertain him with school news. I had stopped working to care for Roy and JD had not yet returned to work. We had support from all sides. People at church handed JD twenty dollar bills to show their concern. When I had visited Roy in the hospital, the administrator had met me in the elevator and assured me there would be no charge for any of his care and any future care if it were needed. The doctors did not send us bills. We appreciated all the unexpected expressions of care and concern.

Roy hadn't complained very much of pain but on September 24th at 6:00PM he cried out, "It hurts". He immediately lapsed into a coma. I carried him to the bedroom. The neighbors took the girls next door. JD called the pediatrician and the minister. All I could do was hold Roy and call his name hoping to reach him. There was no response. I held him and prayed for two hours watching him breathe. Then at 8:00PM his breathing stopped and I knew he was out of my arms and into the arms of God. I just asked, " Dear God, please take care of our little boy".

How would we tell the children that their playmate was gone? Now was the time I needed to pray to God for strength and guidance. With God's help I did the best I could to explain that Roy was now healthy and running around the playground of Heaven. God was taking good care of him and sometime many years from now we would see him again, and he could show us around that beautiful place.

After comforting our children, it was important that we be examples to show them God was with us, and we trusted Him to care for all of us. We still had many things to do and Roy would always be in our hearts.

We did have faith and trust in God but it still was a very difficult time. JD was very quiet. Of course we had tried to console one another, but he hadn't talked to anyone else. Until one day an RCA friend, Williamson, came by for a visit. The floodgates opened and JD talked for about two hours non stop. His friend listened. That was the best thing that could have happened. We had just met another of God's angels, who I'm sure was not aware he had wings.

JD went back to work at RCA in the shop where it was less physical. I returned to part time in the hospital. We found that two children were so many less than three. It did help to have the care of Tommy. He was a busy little angel. First his care expense had helped carry us through a lean time financially and now just having him to care for gave me a responsibility to keep going.

My feeling of being needed was evident in my dreams when one night I met Roy. He was somewhat in the distance but calling me to come to him. I explained that I couldn't come right now. I couldn't leave Karla and Corrine and I knew he was being well cared for. It was nice to see him and kept him close in the family even it was only a dream.

We thought we should have another baby. We already had had three so couldn't have another number three but we could have child number four. The next July 1956 I was again in the delivery room. Our baby girl had just been delivered. Having had an anesthetic and in my half conscious state I met Roy again. I was so thrilled and told him he would be so happy to know he had a little sister, Gayle. He replied, "You don't have to tell me. I picked her out".

We did enjoy our children. Now we had three daughters. We had planned to complete our family by the time we had been married ten years. I had given up on the thought of twelve pregnancies. We had just passed our ninth anniversary. One more year to go, so we had our fourth daughter, Robyn, in August before our tenth anniversary in September. The anesthesiologist exclaimed sadly, "It is a girl and she already has three girls". Dr. Treadwell who knew me well after four deliveries said,

"She doesn't mind. She is just happy to have a healthy baby". I couldn't have said it better myself if I had been fully awake. We had made the plans but God was ever guiding our thoughts.

CHAPTER 4

How much better is it to get wisdom than
gold; and to get understanding rather
than silver! Proverbs 16:16 KJV

I could not imagine where God was leading me next,
but I was willing to hear His suggestions. Looking in the
paper at job opportunities was a regular routine. Not that
I needed a job but you never knew what bit of information
might be found. With a regular position available as
elementary school teacher in Orange, JD had returned to
his original choice of occupation. This was good for the
next twenty-five years.

I saw "RN needed" at Hylond Home for Handicapped
adults and children. It was an ad for a part time night
nurse from 11PM to 7AM. All our children were in school
now so if I worked at night that would not interfere with

the part time St. Joseph position. The children would be asleep and I would be home before JD left so I could get them off to school. Then I could have a peaceful sleep and pretend it was night.

I applied and received the job. It was very interesting, and I was also learning something new as I hadn't worked in this setting before. There were several children with Down Syndrome, and I knew how lovable they tend to be. There were many diagnoses and I used the opportunity to further my knowledge. One thing I learned was that I don't do night shift very well. I had the impression if I worked nights that I could make two days in one. Who really needs to sleep? Not too bright. I didn't work there for long, but it was good experience and one that was evident later that I had been led to answer that ad.

While I was doing part time jobs, God opened a volunteer position as counselor for the World Friendship Girls at Spurgeon Methodist Church. This was a group of teenage girls starting at thirteen years. They were a mission oriented circle that made them a logical stepping stone into the United Methodist Women's organization whose purpose is to support fellowship, and to expand concepts of mission through participation in the global ministries of the church.

Karla, our oldest daughter was turning thirteen and we had three more girls after that so I felt it was sort of my duty to step in as counselor as the former mother was retiring. My experience at Girls' Camp had been so inspirational that I was hoping to give these girls the same kind of opportunity I had received when I was their age.

World Friendship Girls Camp was an event that our two older daughters looked forward to each year and where they renewed friendships over many years. Unfortunately, as often happens, someone with authority decided that girls would not enjoy camp without boys, so it was dissolved and merged with Methodist Youth Fellowship which was a coed group. Therefore our two younger girls did not have the experience. We continued our group in our own church, however, and I remained counselor for about eighteen years.

I depended upon God's guidance for direction in planning programs that the girls would enjoy and receive the fellowship that is so important for young girls and still be a learning experience to further the mission of the church. We visited homes for children and retirement homes for missionaries that were supported by the church. There were retreats at dude ranches in Victorville and Santa Barbara and we chartered a sailboat and captain to sail to Catalina for the weekend. Vacation Village on the bay in San Diego was a retreat where the girls could get away from everyday life, enjoy one another and listen for God's plan for their own lives. Early one morning I wrote this poem:

Friendship Retreat
Away from the chores of the everyday
to seek the peace of God.
Found on the banks of Mission Bay
on the sands where many have trod.

Seek the warming sun in the early morn
Note the sounds of the birds in the air,
Hear the distant boats where the waves are born
Feel the comfort of rest and the ease of care.

Amid the walks, the talks and the boats and bikes,
And lazing in the nice warm sun,
Round the island with friends on nature hikes,
All make it a lot of fun.

With the many shared thoughts under skies of blue
The prayers and the laughter and tears,
Comes the presence of God to our lives anew,
And friendships to last through the years.

In a program sponsored by the mission committee in the church we had Alice Whitney and her adopted

African daughter, Mucizwida, as speakers. Alice Whitney had founded an orphanage called Babyfold in Rhodesia (now Zimbabwe). Mucizwida was nineteen.

In the early years of Babyfold, one of the babies, a newborn orphan was brought in to an already overflowing facility, but Alice could not refuse a tiny orphan baby. They found a place for her, and she was named Mucizwida, which interpreted means "You will love her". She was later legally adopted by Alice and now at nineteen years old had accompanied Alice on this mission trip to the U.S.

God led me to speak to the guests and with World Friendship Girls in mind, to ask how we might assist in the work at Babyfold. We discussed the prospect of the girls being responsible for a portion of Mucizwida (Muchie's) monthly salary. This began a friendship between our girls and Muchie that has continued to this day.

Muchie has retired now and Mother Alice passed away about thirty years ago. As was the African custom, the offspring of the deceased needs to lay flowers on the Mother's grave. Muchie had remained in Africa even Alice had returned to the U.S. Alice was buried at Forest Lawn Cemetery in California. Our World Friendship Girls along with the United Methodist Women and the whole Spurgeon Church collected enough money to bring Muchie to the U.S. so she could complete her required act for her Mother.

Muchie stayed at our house and we traveled around to wherever she needed to go. We enjoyed her visit and she became one of our family--our African daughter and a sister to our other four daughters. She settled into the neighborhood and lived here for five months. You could see her striding down Clinton Avenue to our house, returning from a shopping spree on her own, with her purchases balanced neatly on her head.

Being about six feet tall, Muchie cut quite a figure in the community. She was known by the post office staff as well as the clerks in the 5 and 10 cent store. She is now well passed sixty years old, but she is still one of our family and I feel privileged as she refers to me as Mother. She has lived up to her name of "You will love her". Muchie is still living in Zimbabwe. I look forward to her letters as we continue to correspond by mail. We have been so thankful that God led us to Muchie, or Muchie to us, over fifty years ago.

Since JD was a teacher, I was often asked if I were a teacher also. That had never been one of my ambitions. However, I heard someplace that Santa Ana Junior College was in need of a teacher in the nursing department. Always up for a challenge I had an interview with the head of the department. I was surprised she didn't immediately say, "No, you are not qualified". What she did say was that there was a class for teacher preparation, such as making lesson plans and preparing lectures, at Orange Coast College and if I took that course, she would consider my application.

I did complete the teacher preparation class and was hired at Santa Ana Junior College. I taught in the Vocational Nursing and the Nursing Assistant programs. This was really enjoyable and rewarding working with students in the classroom as well as supervising them on procedures in the clinical setting. I even had the rare privilege and pleasure of instructing our daughter, Gayle, in the LVN program. This also placed me in the State Educational System which began a saving for retirement.

The Sandwich Generation's responsibilities were an apt title for a portion of my twenty-four hour day. My father was not too well and our phone rang frequently for me to go help my mother with his care. That meant hurriedly spanning the two or three miles from our house to theirs. They had lived the same place since I was six months old and Dad had strongly refused to think of moving.

Some would call it coincidence, but to me it was God showing me the way. Our neighbor, also on an acre of land, had moved in triplexes for rentals. There was one available so I again approached my parents with the prospect of selling the house and moving next door to us. My Dad immediately said, "All right, you sell the house". JD and

I got busy and made arrangements and the house sold quickly. The next job was to help them sort, dispose of, sell or retain all their earthly belongings of the past forty-five years in a rather spacious three bedroom home to fit into a three room, one bedroom triplex. It was a good move and we all enjoyed having the grandparents living next door. Their back door and a well-filled candy dish was reached through a gate we made in our side fence.

When I had graduated from nursing school about twenty-five years previously, I received an A.A. degree from Pasadena Junior College and, after State Board exams, an RN. I had dreamed of returning to school to work for a B.S. degree but there just never seemed to be a good time. To my surprise I received a letter from California State College at Fullerton announcing their new nursing program. Maybe this was the time. These coincidences started with a G.

How exciting! This program was accepting the credits earned for the RN as well as the years of nursing experience. It looked like a real possibility. I gathered together all units, letters of reference and verification of experience and applied. I was accepted but realized it would take some divine intervention to pass organic chemistry and statistics along with the rest of the curriculum.

There were only twelve students in that first nursing class. We were known as the "Dirty Dozen". I really enjoyed the other classmates although I was much older than any of them, but they didn't seem to mind. After much prayer and study and twenty-eight years later after an A.A., I graduated receiving a B.S. with honors and also a Public Health Nurse credential. I was quite flattered when the whole country broke out in celebration but soon I discovered that the big event was not my graduation but the 200th birthday of the United States--1976! Oh well, at least my family appreciated my efforts.

With reaching another rung on the ladder, came other opportunities. Since JD was teaching, we would have the same schedule if I were a school nurse. Besides he had suggested it because, as he voiced it, "The school nurse doesn't have to do too much". Now, if a school nurse is reading this, please don't be offended. I soon rearranged his perceptions. I hadn't been in the field more than a week until he humbly ate those words for dinner!

Garden Grove had a need for a school nurse so I accepted a position. My assignment was to be dividing my time among four schools for weekly visits. It was fun to work with the children checking eyes, ears, and any ailments they might have. Home visits were sometimes a challenge but very interesting work. The nurse was invited to give classroom presentations and oversee and discuss the "growing up" films. Some of those sixth graders had more life experiences than I had in my advanced age.

When God led me to work at Hylond Home for handicapped adults and children, I did not know how that would benefit me years later. Mark Twain school had a portion of it's faculty and students delegated to the special needs children. The school nurse position was full time at that one school working mainly with this population. I happened to be the only one who had the experience, small as it was, in that field. The time spent at Mark Twain was the highlight of my career. I was able to really get acquainted with the children. I made frequent rounds to their classrooms and grew to know and love everyone of them and rejoice with what might seem to some people as very small accomplishments but very large to the child and their parents. Sometimes it takes a new learning skill and a great deal of teaching patience to raise a cup from the table to your mouth. That is a cause for celebration. We duly celebrated each new success.

In JD's last year of teaching before retirement there was an opening for school nurse at West Orange School. I had retired from Garden Grove so applied for the job. That was a special time to work with JD. In my evaluation I was jokingly cautioned to not give too much time to Mr. Bradshaw's classroom. JD also viewed first hand that a school nurse cannot be described as "doesn't do too much".

We had lived at Clinton Avenue for thirty years and the children were all grown and in their own homes.

The neighborhood had changed considerably. There were apartments across the street that had once been an orange grove then a nine-hole golf course. Our house had been broken into five times. That should have told us plainly enough that we needed to relocate. We put the house on the market and waited for two years. Finally it was sold to a company to build apartments. That meant that our house would be demolished. As difficult as that thought was, we knew it was the right decision. While we were enjoying our home for those many years, the price of land had increased considerably. The perfect place that we had been led to was now an addition to our retirement fund. I wrote this poem in memory of:

That Old House

You've been our home for thirty years.
Our lives have been your song.
Your memory we'll always keep,
When time has come and gone.

You were just the house we looked for,
The place for kids to grow,
A great big yard, a picket fence,
A pool and lawns to mow.

In birth and death you cared for us
Through laughter, joys and tears.
Your walls rang out with music
That echoed down the years.

You housed the pets so many,
The rabbits, dogs and cats,
Chickens, birds and guinea pigs,
And turtles, mice and rats.

Remember how the little feet
Took shaky first steps on your floors?
How growing girls got so upset
They'd bang and slam your doors?

You watched the children bloom and grow
To ladies from their childhood years
You heard their prayers all through the night
And knew the Lord would still their fears.

When toys and dolls were banished
And to boys the girls did tend
Your porch light gave a signal
That the evening's at an end.

As one by one the daughters
Left the haven of your nest,
From you they wove a new home
With the one that they loved best.

You've now seen many youngsters
With some traits you've seen before,
Come with Mother and with Father
Through your ever welcome door.

How your walls did shake and tremble
With excitement and delight,
As the children brought their children
To come back and spend the night.

From the heritage you gave us,
We will build a home anew,
But we'll evermore be grateful
For the times we've spent with you.

CHAPTER 5

"Now also when I am old and grayheaded, O God, forsake me not until I have shown thy strength unto this generation, and thy power to everyone that is to come". Psalm 71:18 KJV

When we sold the house on Clinton, our next home would include my Mother. She had been living alone since my Father's death nineteen years ago. Now she needed my company and care so we bought a house that the three of us could spread out in and enjoy.

JD was retiring from his twenty-five years teaching at West Orange School. Our main activities were associated with Spurgeon Methodist Church. We drew a circle with a mile radius around the church and found a lovely home that we enjoyed for thirteen years.

After retirement JD was happy to make daily walks around the block with a visit to the church being the halfway mark. He was a regular worker to help the secretary with newsletters, bulletins and sometimes advice on the computer.

During this time, God opened my eyes to a new field in nursing--that of Parish Nurse. I proposed the plan to the church board and was given approval. It was a volunteer position but very rewarding. I had the privilege of visiting the lovely people I had known for years who were now shut-ins. Each week I delivered the taped Sunday message to them and had time for a visit, which kept them in contact with their church and it's congregation. It also was an outlet for nursing for me as we discussed their aches and pains and I felt as if I had not completely retired.

Mother later moved to a convalescent home where I made daily visits. She passed away at the age of ninety-seven. I was fortunate to still have the parish nursing responsibility as there was a huge void in my life without the visits to see Mother.

In 1995 JD's aortic heart valve that had been replaced sixteen years earlier was wearing out. The only remedy was another replacement. He was that much older by now, and it was his decision as to whether to have the surgery or not. Although he knew what was ahead for him, he chose to have it done. His reason was, "Charlotte is not ready for me to leave yet". He was so right! We still had much to do.

In the 1990's God put a hurdle in front of me that I could never have conquered without His help. Since He always had been there when I needed Him I said, "All right but as you know this is an entirely new field". It was Ham radio which had been a way of communication for JD since the 1930's. Now he thought it would be nice for us to have me join him. This meant I had to add another section to my brain or maybe have a brain transplant. I was familiar with stethoscopes, sphygmomanometers, and bedpans but the Morse code with it's dits and dahs, AC's and DC's, Ohms Law, and to find that a "radio wave" was not just a fancy name for raising your hand in farewell was going to be a challenge. However, I bought the rule book and studied diligently to prepare myself to take the test--on receiving code and other fine points of a radio that had always been foreign to me. JD went with me to Long Beach to take the test and was so proud that I only missed one--I thought I had failed because I missed one, but now I had a Ham license and the call letters N6OLX. Then JD gave me perhaps the most heart felt gift he had ever given me (that is beside a lawn mower, electric mixer or a white blouse, which I am happy to say that I was glad to receive those strange gifts and appreciate the fact that he knew I would be. Some people received diamond necklaces but he knew that wouldn't be my choice). He presented me with my very own 2 Meter radio. That meant from now on whenever I went someplace and he was at home or if he was at one end of the mall and I was at the other, by calling "WB6J this is N6OLX" we were in direct communication. We enjoyed our forerunner to texting for many years until the time came when we no longer went separate ways. I might even learn to text before I'm a hundred.

JD's surgery and convalescence went well but as he remarked, "When you are taken down, you never come back up quite as high". He was walking with a cane now but in good spirits and still enjoying life. Ever listening for direction, we found our time had come to downsize. We gave everything that they would take to the children and moved to a condominium across from the church. We were there for four years but questioned that if something happened to me, who would continue to care for JD?

With the caregiver question in mind and much to the chagrin of our daughters, we decided to move to Park Plaza, which was a retirement home with assisted living. This was about as downsize as we could get, but it was good. JD's world consisted of all of the facility and friends with whom he readily became acquainted. Our meals were provided. I started some cooking classes and led Sunday services of Uplifting Thoughts for the residents.

We were there for six years. I was finding the need to do more and more that JD was not able to do. As he and I discussed our situation, we rationalized that I was doing all the assisting, and we were not using the amenities of the facility Our funds were diminishing too quickly, so we chose to move to a regular apartment, and I could do what I was already doing with less expense. By this time JD had gone from using a cane to a walker and now a wheelchair.

I searched for an apartment in the vicinity of a hospital, doctor's office and convalescent home. Just being prepared for whatever came next. The telephone was my way of searching until I found what was a good possibility. Then Gayle visited the place and gave her approval, so we said, "That is the place" and made arrangements to move. This time it took a whole band of angels consisting of children, grandchildren and friends of grandchildren to move only a short distance to Meridian Apartments. We moved in, sight unseen, but were happy with the decision.

We settled into our new place but JD was getting increasingly more weak. I was now giving twenty-four hour total care. I know it was so hard for JD, but his only complaint was, "You have to do so much for me". I tried to assure him that it wasn't too much because I loved him. I was so thankful that as a nurse I could give him good care, and I was being given the strength to do it. The only problem I had was when he fell. Although he was using his walker, which he could use with my assistance, he still fell and the paramedics came to help get him up and back to bed.

As the days went on, I was able to get some help from hospice to obtain supplies and a hospital bed. By that time he was confined to bed. Then my dilemma was how to get him from our bed to the hospital bed in the living room. I could not support his total weight and I was afraid he would fall again.

God was watching out for us. When I couldn't imagine how I would manage to transfer JD from one bed to another, two angels named Sharon and Bob came to the rescue and the mission was accomplished.

JD's last days were spent with children, grandchildren and great grandchildren making frequent visits and I was always there. Days and nights were all the same except we didn't eat at night. Sleeping was sporadic. I slept in bits and snatches in the recliner by the bed. As I knew the end was coming soon, I prayed for emotional strength and told JD, "If you have to go before I do, I'll be all right". It was so hard to let him go, but I loved him too much to ask him to stay and be miserable. His way of saying goodbye was by matter-of-factly declaring, "I love you and I know you love me. That's all that matters". We prayed the "Lord's Prayer" together and I knew the God that we were speaking to was very close. On August 6, 2007 our vow to be true to each other" 'til death do us part" was completed. Nearly fifty-nine years ago in a short ceremony I had become a wife and now in the twinkling of an eye I was transformed into a widow. God continued to be with me to keep the promise I made to JD that, "I will be all right". That day N6OLX became idle and WB6J became silent.

I thought a lot about what "all right" is. JD knew me as a person who was always doing something even if I did it wrong, had an interest in learning new things, and basically had a positive attitude. Therefore, he would want me to remain the person he loved.

While I was pondering on what would keep me all right, I tripped on a crack in the sidewalk and everything went all wrong. I tried to keep from falling flat on my face so braced myself with my arms. I guess there is no way to fall right, but the angels are all around us. A lovely angel lady stopped her car in the middle of Memory Lane and came to my rescue helping me up and driving me home. The right rotator cuff in my shoulder was not happy. It required surgery and then extended physical therapy. At first this seemed like irreparable, however, God continued to be by my side and gave me the strength I needed, as well as, making me realize how important exercise is. This knowledge convinced me to continue in daily exercise even to this day.

After that brief interlude, I still questioned what I could do to learn something new? The answer was to take a college course. I had no transportation but everyone talked about online and I had no online. I needed a computer. Daughter, Robyn, took me to make the purchase of an Apple MacBook. Then the next obstacle to tackle was to learn how to "compute". Robyn very patiently overlooked my ignorance and answered all my stupid questions. Finally I learned enough to be somewhat efficient and able to communicate in the 20th century. I still haven't conquered the technology in the 21st century but I haven't given up.

With my newly acquired knowledge, I checked on colleges. Feeling more confident with the telephone, I called a college that looked promising. They connected me with an advisor to assist prospective students. After our introductions, her first question was, "When did you graduate from high school?" When my answer was "1944," I thought we had been disconnected. There was a long pause, then she hesitantly replied, "I'm sorry we are not qualified to work with anyone over seventy-five". I didn't wait for further explanation. I decided there must be a better way.

gmail was fairly familiar so I continued to explore that medium. You know those little ads that pop up in front of you whether you want them to or not? One really caught my eye that sounded exactly what I was looking for. It was the Institute of Integrative Nutrition (IIN). Their premise was to promote good health by eating healthy foods like whole grains, good fats, fruits and vegetables and drinking water. I was especially impressed that they proclaimed a holistic approach. Good health is being healthy in body, mind and spirit.

I made up my mind to try using the telephone again. I still wasn't completely comfortable with just the information found on the computer. When I reached IIN, a lovely person answered. My first question was, "Is there a maximum age limit for your students?" She assured me there was not. She answered all my questions and convinced me that I did know enough about a computer to be successful. I was still doubtful but I signed on for the year course.

Once again I had been led to the right place. I completed the program and graduated with a certificate declaring me to be a Health Counselor. I did not pursue health counseling as a new career. My interest was in encouraging other older persons who were in a similar circumstance to mine to have a lively interest in life and find avenues to explore and a reason to "wake up and smile".

My website says that to wake up and smile leads to a gladness heart. That phrase, Gladness Heart, came to me many years ago out of the blue.

It goes like this:

> Yesterday has passed away,
> God has our tomorrows.
> Take today and do your part,
> As your part is given.
> That's the way to gladness heart,
> That's the road to Heaven.

Being a graduate from the Institute of Integrative Nutrition I used my health counseling technique to volunteer to give a talk on "Wake Up and Smile" at Park Plaza, our former retirement residence. The following is the information I presented to them:

"You may wonder why anyone would want to wake up and smile when they don't even want to smile first thing in the morning. I would not advocate doing what a friend of mine did in response to the suggestion that, "you need to smile five times everyday". So she said, "I look in the mirror first thing and smile five times. That's it for the day".I think she missed the point.

What happens when you smile? The corners of your mouth turn upward and that exercises your facial muscles. That begins your morning exercises on a happy note. If you continue to smile you may develop laugh wrinkles. You're probably going to get wrinkles anyway so they may as well be happy wrinkles. Now you are ready to do whatever kind of exercise that will begin your day. Even if it is just deep breathing, that is good.

To even wake up in the morning is a huge privilege. How wonderful to look ahead for twenty-four hours and know that you have the ability to choreograph this day into a unique and beautiful dance never seen before. When you greet people with a "good morning", you can really mean it is a "good" morning. As you question, "How are you?" you can sincerely care about their response. If a smile accompanies these greetings, you are very likely to receive one in return.

It is not imperative that you be on the go constantly. Your added years have given you the privilege to occasionally sit back in a comfortable chair and let your mind wander into Memoryland. I think of memories as the whipped cream on top of life's slice of pie. Turn your everyday conscious thoughts off and relish the events that have made up your life.

When I am luxuriating in Memoryland, I like to look far down the long hall from whence I came and one by one open the doors on either side of the passage. I approach the first door cautiously and turn the knob. I enter the room to be greeted by a breathtaking view of gorgeous mountains. I'm reminded of the dreamy Smoky Mountains, the majestic Rocky Mountains and also many hills like Daffodil Hill that were spectacular. In addition there are the seashores--the Pacific and Atlantic coastlines, and the fall leaves of the north east. All of these we had visited over the years.

As I listen at the next door, I hear children's laughter. I can't wait to swing that door open and see my family of children. Some are ours and some are ones I cared for in the absence of their parents. I hear the babble of infants and the sweet cherubic voices of the toddlers as they are introduced to the familiar strains of "Jesus Loves Me" or "Jesus Wants Me for a Sunbeam". From the time I was fifteen and for sixty years I cared for the infants and toddlers in the church nursery during worship time. I saw children come back years later with their children and I was even there for the grandchildren. What a privilege it was to have shared in so many young lives as they received their first experiences in the love and joy in God's house. I also heard the enthusiastic shouts of youngsters returning home from school, even some rebellious outbursts of frustrated teenagers, and then the whispered confidences of wide-eyed first loves. Those all blended together into a beautiful symphony of exuberant young life.

As I proceed down the hall, I notice the next entrance is decorated with a heart. My own heart swells as I peer expectantly inside. That one takes me back many years. I can feel again the joy and anticipation of a young sailor coming to call, the joy of having that special person to learn to know, to trust, and realize that this is the one with whom I wish to spend the rest of my life. and, yes, as we predicted, we did celebrate our fiftieth anniversary and beyond. I can close my eyes and again feel the comfort of his strong arms around me and appreciate those many loving years we spent together.

There are many more doors along the hall but I may save those for another time. That is a long, long hall representing eighty-seven years. I have no fear of opening any of those doors and examining what is inside. Memories are an important aspect of our lives. We can either dwell on them to the exclusion of everything else or can enjoy them to enhance our lives of today by capitalizing on the knowledge we have gained and life experiences we can bring to share with others. Those memories are ours and only ours because we are unique individuals".

After giving this talk and inspired by the response of the residents, I considered what I might do to reach out to others with the same kind of message. God was one step ahead of me again. I received an email that the graduates of IIN were invited to join a class to "Launch Your Dreambook". This looked like the next step to continue following God's lead. It remains to be seen what the outcome of this adventure will be.

With this class we are given encouragement and instruction on writing the book of our choice, how to get it published, and then actually launching that dreambook. It is a five month course in progress.

I am so thankful that I have my four daughters living near by. Karla takes me to church. Corrine comes as often as she can. She lives a little further away. Gayle phones every morning. Robyn visits once a week. Besides there are frequent phone calls just as the spirit moves them. When there is time in their busy schedules I enjoy visits with the sons-in-law, grandchildren and great grandchildren, too. I try not to expect too much of the family. It makes me happy to see them enjoying their individual families. Now is their time. It also is important to maintain friendships. This I do with a group of longtime friends from church (mostly widows) whom I join weekly for dinner out and usually a lengthy visit and sometimes get-togethers in between.

It is comforting to know that God is still sending His angels to watch over those of us who are in the unorphaned category. Just last spring I had an appointment at a Wellness class about a half mile from home. My mode of transportation is walking. The only problem was a fierce Santana wind blowing. I decided it wasn't far, so I walked out the door. As long as I had a wall, building or tree to hold on to I was able to stagger along. However, I came to a place where there was nothing but open space. A tornado type gust of wind slammed against me and to prevent landing ungracefully on the ground I managed to cautiously lower myself to a patch of grass. Then I couldn't resist the force of the wind to stand up, so I just sat there hoping the wind would die down a little. Suddenly a hand the size of three of mine reached out to me and the owner said, "Can I help you?" He had such a kind voice and smile that I trustingly accepted his offer of assistance, and reached for his hand--there weren't a lot of choices. Apparently he worked for the post office as he pushed his cart with one hand and his other was supporting mine as we walked the rest of the way to deliver me to the door of my destination. I have no idea who he was but as he turned to go, I was sure I heard the rush of the wind in his wings as a mighty gust blew him back in the direction from whence we came. I never described this incident to my family for fear they would have their aged mother committed to an institution for the mentally incompetent for heading out on foot in a 90 mile an hour wind on such a very blustery day. However, I really appreciated the man who was friendly and strong enough to stand up against the wind, and his wings looked like they had been well used.

As I reflect on these seventy years since I placed my letter to God at the foot of the tiny man made cross in the mountains, I again thank the lovely Christian lady who provided the fifteen dollars that made it possible. She had no idea of the far reaching influence that kind act made on the life of one young impressionable girl who tried to live as Micah in the Old Testament wrote simply in chapter 6, the 8th verse, "What doth the Lord require of thee, but to do justly, and to love mercy, and to walk humbly with thy God"

Everyday we are making decisions. I have often thought of how different my life might have been if I had chosen another path up the mountain of life. My decisions were made with God as my counselor and guide. When I gave Him control of my life I trusted He would help me make the right choices. There have been rough places when I have tripped, stubbed my toes and been buffeted about in a storm, but he didn't promise to make life easy only that He would always face life with me. I thanked Him for His care at those times, as well as, the smooth terrain when I could run merrily singing along the pathway. I plan to continue walking merrily, though perhaps a little more slowly, but follow in His footsteps to whatever adventures still remain for me to experience until He leads me to the mountaintop and the end of my journey. There I will catch my first glimpse of JD in the distance waiting to welcome me with open arms to our new home--what a joyful reunion that will be. I wonder, will he again carry me over the threshold as he did so long ago?